# THE DEADLIEST
# DINOSAURS

BY **"DINO" DON LESSEM**

ILLUSTRATIONS BY **JOHN BINDON**

**LERNER PUBLICATIONS COMPANY / MINNEAPOLIS**

W

*To Hall Train, one of the least nasty and most talented of all dinosaur people*

At present, only a few fossils exist of *Megaraptor*, *Pyroraptor*, and *Variraptor*. In depicting these dinosaurs, the artist drew from the fossil evidence and from what is known of the appearance of other similar dinosaurs.

Photographs courtesy of: © Denis Finnin, American Museum of Natural History, p. 17; © Francois Gohier, p. 28; © Ron Timblin, Dino Don, Inc., p. 29.

*This book is available in two editions:*
Library binding by Lerner Publications Company,
    a division of Lerner Publishing Group
Soft cover by First Avenue Editions,
    an imprint of Lerner Publishing Group
241 First Avenue North
Minneapolis, MN 55401 U.S.A.

Website address: www.lernerbooks.com


Library of Congress Cataloging-in-Publication-Data

Lessem, Don.
    The deadliest dinosaurs / by Don Lessem ; illustrations by John Bindon.
        p.   cm. — (Meet the dinosaurs)
    Includes index.
        ISBN: 0-8225-1421-4 (lib. bdg. : alk. paper)
        ISBN: 0-8225-2619-0 (pbk. : alk. paper)
        1. Dinosaurs—Juvenile literature. I. Bindon, John, ill. II. Title. III. Series: Lessem, Don. Meet the dinosaurs.
    QE861.5.L4755 2005
    567.912—dc22                                                    2004011282

Manufactured in the United States of America
1 2 3 4 5 6 - JR - 10 09 08 07 06 05

# TABLE OF CONTENTS

# MEET THE
# DEADLIEST DINOSAURS

**WELCOME, DINOSAUR FANS!**

I'm "Dino" Don. I LOVE dinosaurs. I even love deadly dinosaurs. Raptors were the scariest, deadliest dinosaurs of all. I'm just glad we were not alive when they were! Come see them here. It's safe to look.

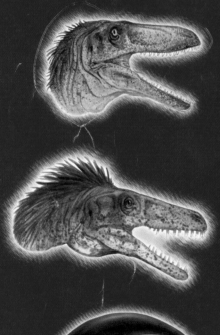

**DEINONYCHUS (dy-NAWN-ih-kuhs)**
Length: 12 feet
Home: western North America
Time: 115 million years ago

**DROMAEOSAURUS (DROH-mee-oh-SAWR-uhs)**
Length: 6 feet
Home: western North America
Time: 76 million years ago

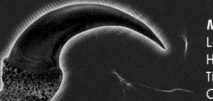

**MEGARAPTOR (MEHG-uh-RAP-tohr)**
Length: 26 feet
Home: South America
Time: 86 million years ago
Only parts of its leg and giant arm claw have been found.

**MICRORAPTOR** (MY-kroh-RAP-tohr)
Length: 1.8 feet
Home: Asia
Time: 124 million years ago

**PYRORAPTOR** (PY-roh-RAP-tohr)
Length: 5.5 feet
Home: western Europe
Time: 69 million years ago

**UTAHRAPTOR** (YOO-tah-RAP-tohr)
Length: 20 feet
Home: western North America
Time: 125 million years ago

**VARIRAPTOR** (VAHR-ih-RAP-tohr)
Length: 8.3 feet
Home: western Europe
Time: 71 million years ago

**VELOCIRAPTOR** (veh-LAHS-ih-RAP-tohr)
Length: 6.5 feet
Home: Asia
Time: 80 million years ago

# VERY DEADLY DINOSAURS

One of the deadliest of all dinosaurs is hunting. Its name is *Utahraptor.* It's almost as big as an ice cream truck. And it has huge claws and sharp teeth. Running quickly, *Utahraptor* chases after a huge plant-eating dinosaur.

The plant eater is nearly as long as a tennis court. That's longer than three *Utahraptor*. It probably weighs as much as 10 of them. But the plant eater is helpless against the killer claws and teeth of this very deadly dinosaur.

# THE TIME OF THE DEADLIEST DINOSAURS

*Utahraptor*

*Deinonychus*

125 million
years ago

115 million
years ago

*Utahraptor* and its relatives are the most deadly dinosaurs known. Some people call them **raptor dinosaurs.** Raptor dinosaurs lived 125 million to 65 million years ago. Most of them were small meat eaters. Like other meat eaters, raptors had sharp, killing teeth.

Velociraptor

Dromaeosaurus

Pyroraptor

80 million
years ago

76 million
years ago

69 million
years ago

But these deadly dinosaurs were different from other meat-eating dinosaurs. Raptor dinosaurs had huge curved claws. They used their claws to slice their **prey,** the animals they hunted and ate. And raptors had long, rodlike tails. Their tails might have helped them balance while they chased prey.

# DINOSAUR FOSSIL FINDS

The numbers on the map on page 11 show some of the places where people have found fossils of the dinosaurs in this book. You can match each number on the map to the name and picture of the dinosaurs on this page.

**1. Deinonychus**    **2. Dromaeosaurus**    **3. Megaraptor**    **4. Microraptor**

**5. Pyroraptor**    **6. Utahraptor**    **7. Variraptor**    **8. Velociraptor**

Raptors and other dinosaurs died out millions of years ago. All that we know about them comes from **fossils.** Fossils are traces left by animals and plants that have died. Scientists have found fossils of raptor dinosaur bones, teeth, and claws mostly on the northern continents.

Fossils help scientists understand what raptor dinosaurs looked like and how they lived. Fossils of claws and jaws also help scientists figure out which dinosaurs were the deadliest. The deadliest dinosaurs had killer claws and powerful jaws.

Fossils show us that some raptor dinosaurs were tiny, as small as puppies. Others were as long as two cars. But none were even half the size of a big meat eater like *Tyrannosaurus rex*. Why were some raptor dinosaurs so small?

Scientists think they had a special job in nature. Small raptors such as *Pyroraptor* probably hunted lizards, small animals, and other little dinosaurs. Raptors that ate such small prey couldn't grow very large.

Size doesn't matter when it comes to nastiness. Raptors were deadly hunters, no matter how big they were. And by teaming up, small raptors could take on animals much bigger than they were.

Some raptor dinosaurs were even deadly to each other. One baby *Velociraptor* fossil was found with tooth marks in its head. Another *Velociraptor* might have killed it!

# KILLER
# CLAWS AND JAWS

We are in the desert of east central Asia 80 million years ago. A *Velociraptor* is attacking a *Protoceratops*. Suddenly, the sand dune they are standing on caves in. The fighting dinosaurs are both buried in the sand.

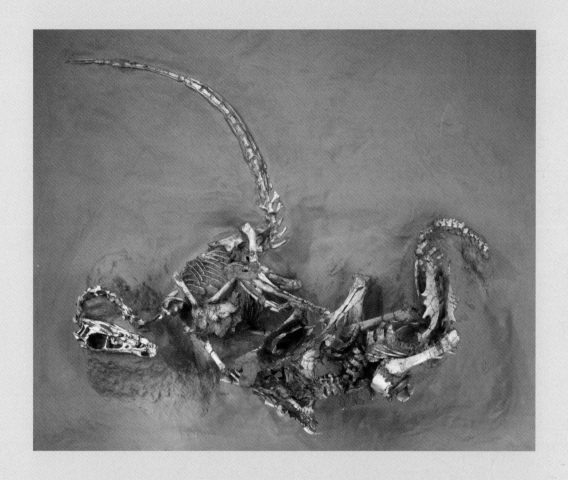

Researchers found fossils of these two dinosaurs in 1971. The **skeletons** were nearly complete. The dinosaurs were found in the same position they were in when they died. Their fossils showed scientists how raptors used their deadly claws and jaws.

The claws on a raptor's hands and feet
were its biggest weapon. Raptor claws
were curved and sharp to hook into prey.
Raptors had one giant claw on each limb.
They could pull back the claw just as a cat
pulls back its claws. That way, raptors could
run without dragging their huge claws.

When a raptor caught up to its prey, it jumped and swiped. It slashed with its hands and feet. Its claws sliced open its victim. No dinosaur had deadlier weapons.

A little *Variraptor* has trapped a tiny animal. With a single leap and bite, the raptor crushes and swallows the animal's head.

*Variraptor* had small, narrow jaws filled with
pointed teeth. Each tooth had grooves like
those on a steak knife for sawing through
meat. *Variraptor* could tear even a larger
animal in two.

Raptors, such as these human-sized *Deinonychus*, might have hunted in groups called **packs.** This pack has come across an injured *Gastonia*, a large armored dinosaur.

*Deinonychus* is quick enough to dart in and around the dying dinosaur. Several *Deinonychus* use their claws to attack the armored dinosaur. They slash at its soft belly with their huge, sharp claws. Together, the raptors will finish off their prey.

# RAPTOR DISCOVERIES

The first raptor ever discovered was *Dromaeosaurus*. Its fossils were found in western Canada in 1914. *Dromaeosaurus* was no bigger than a golden retriever but had a much longer tail.

*Dromaeosaurus* was a smart hunter. And its teeth were sharp, with ridges for slicing meat. Other raptors had the same type of teeth. But *Dromaeosaurus* had an unusually wide, strong head for its size.

In 2000, the discovery of *Microraptor* in China excited scientists all over the world. *Microraptor* is one of the smallest dinosaurs ever found. It was no bigger than a crow.

*Microraptor* was also closely related to
birds. But it was a nasty dinosaur with sharp
claws. We don't know for sure what it ate.
Perhaps it hunted lizards, tiny animals,
insects, or even birds!

Scientist Jim Kirkland found a fossil of the largest raptor dinosaur in 1991. Dr. Kirkland's team dug up the huge claw of a *Utahraptor*.

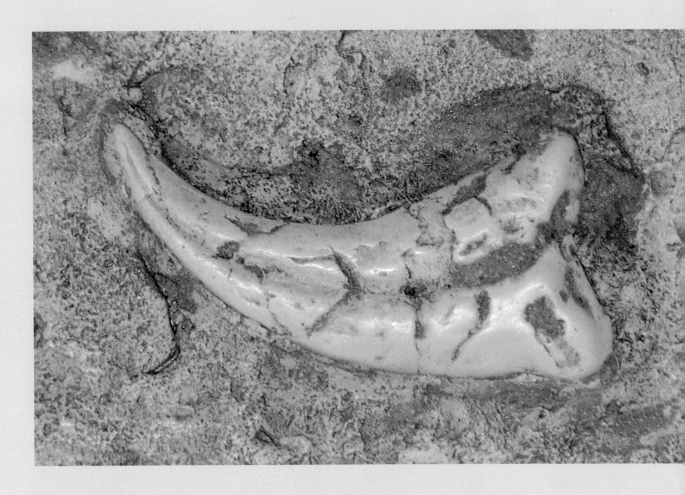

*Utahraptor* was a fast and deadly hunter. Its toe claw was razor sharp and longer than your foot. *Utahraptor* also had sharp teeth, good eyes, and strong legs. Perhaps *Utahraptor* was the deadliest dinosaur of them all.

Imagine a killer dinosaur as long as a
school bus, with claws twice as long as a
banana! Such a frightening creature lived
in South America 86 million years ago. Its
name was *Megaraptor*. It could have
hunted huge prey like this *Rebbachisaurus*.

Most of what we know about *Megaraptor*
comes from one fossil leg and a huge claw.
But scientists hope to discover more.
*Megaraptor* probably isn't closely related
to true raptor dinosaurs.  But it was still one
deadly, giant-clawed dinosaur!

# GLOSSARY

**fossils (FAH-suhlz):** the remains, tracks, or traces of something that lived long ago

**packs (PAKS):** small groups of animals that live, eat, and travel together

**prey (PRAY):** animals that other animals hunt and eat

**raptor (RAP-tohr) dinosaurs:** meat-eating dinosaurs with a killer claw on each foot and long rodlike tails

**skeleton (SKEH-luh-tihn):** the framework of bones in the body

# INDEX